GROUNDWATER D.

Groundwater Dams
for Small-scale Water Supply

Åke Nilsson

Practical Action Publishing Ltd
25 Albert Street, Rugby, CV21 2SD, Warwickshire, UK
www.practicalactionpublishing.com

© Intermediate Technology Publications 1988

First published 1988\Digitised 2013

ISBN 10: 185339050X
ISBN 13: 9781853390500
ISBN Library Ebook: 9781780442297
Book DOI: http://dx.doi.org/10.3362/9781780442297

Since 1974, Practical Action Publishing has published and
disseminated books and information in support of international
development work throughout the world. Practical Action
Publishing is a trading name of Practical Action Publishing Ltd
(Company Reg. No. 1159018), the wholly owned publishing
company of Practical Action. Practical Action Publishing trades
only in support of its parent charity objectives and any profits are
covenanted back to Practical Action (Charity Reg. No. 247257,
Group VAT Registration No. 880 9924 76).

Contents

LIST OF FIGURES

Preface

This text is an updated version of a report on groundwater dams published by The Royal Institute of Technology, Stockholm in 1984. It presents the results of a literature study combined with study visits to Africa and India. The study has been financed by the Swedish Agency for Research Cooperation with Developing Countries (SAREC) to which I hereby express my gratitude.

I am grateful to Professor Gert Knutsson, Department of Land Improvement and Drainage, The Royal Institute of Technology, for his support and guidance. I also want to thank all colleagues and friends I have met in Africa and India who have so willingly supplied information and guided me in the field. In this respect I am especially indebted to staff of MAJI, Tanzania; DNA and GEOMOC, Mozambique; Ministry of Water Development and the Machakos Integrated Development Programme, Kenya; and the Central Ground Water Board, the Tamil Nadu Agricultural University, and the Tamil Nadu Forest Department, India. I owe special thanks to Professor Otto Wipplinger, Stellenbosch, South Africa, for sending me the details of his great knowledge and experience. Figures have been drawn by Mr Giles Francis, Trivandrum. The author and publishers are grateful to sources referred to under the illustrations.

Åke Nilsson
Trivandrum, September, 1987.

Chapter 1
INTRODUCTION

Supplying safe water and sanitation to all by 1990 is the target of the International Drinking Water Supply and Sanitation Decade. It is clear that this will not be reached, and the work will continue for several decades to come. Experience has shown that there has to be an orientation away from expensive, sophisticated techniques towards appropriate, low-cost and socially acceptable techniques that are adapted to local conditions.

Many developing countries are located in climatic regions where rainfall is seasonal and highly erratic. Supplying water in such regions is to a large extent a matter of storing water from the rainy season to the dry season, and from years with high rainfall to dry years. Using groundwater is a way of overcoming the seasonal shortages, but in some areas even the groundwater resources are depleted towards the end of the dry season and in many areas there are no aquifers available, or they would require deep-drilled wells and pumps for development, a fact that makes this alternative less suitable in certain socio-economic environments.

A method of storing water which has received considerable attention during the last few years is the use of groundwater dams. Damming groundwater for conservation purposes is not a new concept. Groundwater dams were constructed on the island of Sardinia in Roman times and structures in Tunisia show that damming of groundwater was practised by old civilizations in North Africa. There is a report of a sand-storage dam built in Arizona in the eighteenth century. More recently, various small-scale groundwater damming techniques have been developed and applied in many parts of the world, notably in India, southern and East Africa, and Brazil.

1. Definitions
A conventional dam for water storage is usually built across a river or a stream, and collects surface water which is stored in the open reservoir upstream of the dam. *A groundwater dam obstructs the flow of groundwater and stores water below*

1

the ground surface. It may also serve as a collecting structure that diverts groundwater flow, for instance to recharge adjacent aquifers, or it can raise the groundwater table in an aquifer with a limited flow of groundwater, which is thus made accessible for pumping.

Groundwater dams may be of two types, sub-surface dams and sand-storage dams. A *sub-surface dam* is constructed below ground level and arrests the flow in a natural aquifer, whereas a *sand-storage dam* impounds water in sediments caused to accumulate by the dam itself.

The general principle of a sub-surface dam is shown in Figure 1.1. An aquifer consisting of permeable alluvial sediments in a small valley supplies water to a village by means of a shallow dug well. The area has a monsoon climate, and due to consumption and the natural groundwater flow, the aquifer used to be drained out during the dry season and consequently the well dried up. To prevent this, a trench has been dug across the valley, reaching down to bedrock. An impervious wall has been constructed in the trench, which has then been refilled with the excavated material. The reservoir will be recharged during the monsoon period and the stored water can be used during the dry season. Excess groundwater will flow above the dam crest and recharge downstream aquifers.

Figure 1.1. General principle of a sub-surface dam.

2

The general principle of a sand-storage dam is shown by the example in Figure 1.2. The villagers used to collect their water from the small non-perennial stream at times when it carried water, or from holes dug in the shallow river bed for a short period after the rains. The quantity of water stored was not sufficient to supply water to the village during the entire dry period. By the construction of a weir of suitable height across the stream bed, sand carried by heavy flows during the rains has been deposited and the reservoir has filled up with sand. This artificial aquifer will be replenished each year during the rains, and water will be stored for use during the dry season.

Figure 1.2. General principle of a sand-storage dam.

By using this method it is often possible to extract water by gravity from the reservoir by using a pipe through the dam wall, thus avoiding the construction of a well and the problem of pump installation and maintenance.

A groundwater dam can also be a combination of the two types. When constructing a sub-surface dam in a river bed, one can increase the storage volume by letting the dam wall rise over the surface, thus causing additional accumulation of sediments. Similarly, when a sand-storage dam is constructed it is usually necessary to excavate a trench in the sand bed in order to reach bedrock or a stable, impervious layer.

2. Advantages

The advantages of using groundwater dams instead of common surface storage are many. Evaporation losses are reduced or even completely avoided and once constructed, the designed storage will be available for a very long time and not, as in the case of surface reservoirs, subject to reduction caused by siltation and vegetal growth.

The water stored is less susceptible to pollution, and health hazards such as mosquito breeding and spreading of snail fever are avoided.

When conventional surface storage is used, it means that land is occupied for the reservoir; in the case of groundwater dams the land above the stored water can be used for other purposes.

3. Experience

This study presents the result of a literature survey combined with field visits to some sites in Africa and India where groundwater dams have been constructed and proposed. Most of the collected literature consists of specific reports from isolated projects. Two references describe more general studies presenting experience from Namibia and French-speaking Africa. The present text does not, although it covers experience from many parts of the world, pretend to be exhaustive in any respect. It presents general conclusions in the introductory chapters and finally some of the field projects are described. For details the reader is referred to the original documents which are all included in the list of references. The main subject is the storage of groundwater for small-scale water supply in developing countries. Groundwater dams for the protection of aquifers or sub-surface works, or such technical solutions that are developed and especially adapted for climatic and technological conditions typical for industrialized countries, are not treated in any depth.

Figure 1.3 shows a map of the world where all groundwater dam construction sites identified under this study have been marked. Most of the sites and areas have been described in the following text, and notably in Chapter 6.

The interest in using groundwater dams for water supply has increased during the last few years in connection with rural development projects, and several research projects are

4

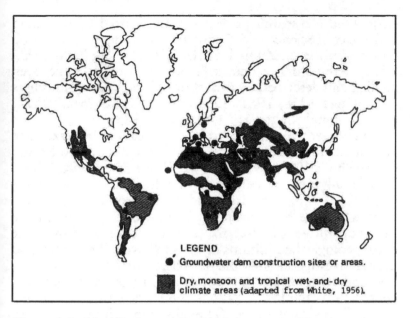

Figure 1.3. Identified groundwater dam construction areas.

planned or have already started in Asia, Africa and South America.

The Central Ground Water Board of India has sited and constructed a number of sub-surface dams in Kerala, and regional suitability plans for an area in South India have been prepared under a research project at the Royal Institute of Technology, Stockholm (Ahnfors, 1980; Destouni and Johansson, 1987; Nilsson, 1987). The research project has also tested and developed simple techniques for the hydrogeological investigations that should preceed the construction of groundwater dams. Using groundwater dams for water storage is now a widely accepted technique in South India; several dams have already been constructed by state irrigation and forest departments, and large-scale application is planned in connection with present water harvesting and drought relief programmes.

Several dams have been built during the last few years in Ethiopia by government departments with technical and financial support from Sweden (Hansson and Nilsson, 1986). UNESCO has supported the construction of some dams in

5

Africa and a research project is being started by the Lund University of Science and Technology, Sweden, in cooperation with authorities in Zimbabwe (UNESCO, 1984; Bjelm et.al., 1986). Sand-storage dam schemes in Namibia have been studied and described by Professor O.Wipplinger and others (Wipplinger 1958, 1961, 1965 and 1982; Aubroeck, 1971; Beaumont and Kluger, 1973; Stengel, 1968).

Comprehensive studies and field applications in Brazil have been made by Institute de Pesquisas Tecnológicas do Estado de Sao Pãulo (IPT, 1981 and 1982; Oliveira and Leife, 1984).

Generally it can be concluded that the present experience is positive; if properly sited and built, groundwater dams definitely serve their purpose. Some words of caution are needed, however. Before constructing a dam, the hydrogeological conditions at the site have to be known and proper investigations should be carried out. At the same time, the total costs have to be kept to an absolute minimum and consequently the investigations should be done with simple and inexpensive methods. Generalisations within areas with similar conditions should be used whenever possible. Caution is also needed during construction; it has to be properly planned according to seasonal conditions, appropriate materials should be used, and basic engineering practices should be followed.

It is also important to stress that groundwater damming is not a universally applicable method for water supply. It can be applied only if certain physical conditions are at hand and it should be looked upon more as an alternative when water supply cannot be arranged more easily with conventional methods.

Chapter 2
PHYSICAL CONDITIONS

1. Climate
The need to dam groundwater for water supply purposes is caused basically by the irregularity of rainfall. In arid areas every drop of water is valuable and should be saved. In monsoon-climate areas the total amount of rainfall would generally be sufficient to cater to the needs of people and agriculture, but here the seasonality means that during some parts of the year water is not available. Damming groundwater is thus a means of bridging over the seasonal dry periods. In addition, quite often the monsoon rains also fail and this can have a disastrous effect on the water-supply situation.

Damming of groundwater may also be done in climatic regions where water is available throughout the year, but where one wishes to increase the quantity or raise the groundwater level in the aquifer actually dammed, or in surrounding or underlying aquifers.

All dry, monsoon and tropical wet-and-dry climate areas of the world have been marked on the map in Figure 1.3. These are the parts of the world where the rainfall conditions are most suited for damming groundwater and there is a good correspondence with the actual groundwater dam sites.

Arid areas of the world are by Köppen's definition those where the potential evaporation is larger than rainfall. The relative advantage of damming groundwater as compared to common surface storage depends to a large extent on the losses that would result from open-surface evaporation. Some values of potential evaporation from relevant areas where groundwater dams have been constructed or proposed are presented in Table 2.1.

It is evident that evaporation losses from open water surfaces in these areas are considerable. The loss of say 2 metres from a reservoir may represent quite a large portion of its total capacity.

Depending upon the level of the groundwater table and the capillarity of the aquifer material, there is some limited evaporation also from groundwater. The evaporation of water

7

Table 2.1. Rainfall and potential evaporation data from some dry areas.

Area	Average rainfall (mm/year)	Potential evaporation (mm/year)	Reference
Biskra, Algeria	180	1,330	UN, 1973
Tarfaya, Morocco	110	850	UN, 1973
Moudjéria, Mauritania	170	1,870	UN, 1973
Lugh Ferrandi, Somalia	360	2,060	UN, 1973
North Turkana, Kenya	200-600	>2,500	Sørlie, 1978
Machakos, Kenya	850	1,600-1,800	Fellows and Fridfeldt, 1983
Dodoma, Tanzania	590	1,110	UN, 1973
Catuane, Mozambique	670	1,300	UN, 1973
Gross Barmen, Namibia	400	2,260	Hellwig, 1973
Palghat Gap, India	2,000-3,000	1,550	Central Ground Water Board, 1980
Bartlett Dam, Arizona	350	3,090	Skibitzke et al., 1961
Nordeste, Brazil	500-1,000	2,000	IPT, 1981

from sand has been studied quantitatively by Hellwig (1973) at experiments at Swakop River in Namibia. The evaporation from a saturated sand surface was found to be approximately 8 per cent less than from an open water surface. The lowering of the water table by 0.3m below the sand surface reduced the evaporation from a fine sand to 50 per cent of that from an open water surface. The corresponding figure when keeping the water level at 0.6m depth in medium sand was 10 per cent. The relation between evaporation and depth of water table is shown in Figure 2.1. The sorting of the material has an influence on the extent of evaporation losses. It was found that a reduction of particles of less than 0.1mm diameter from 9 per cent to 0.7 per cent in a layer of medium sand, reduced evaporation by 25 per cent at 0.30 metres depth to the water table. It is important therefore that the accumulation of fine particles at shallow depths in sand-storage dams is avoided. Evaporation as a function of particle size is shown in Figure 2.2.

2. Topography
The topographical conditions govern to a large extent the technical possibilities of constructing the dams as well as achieving sufficiently large storage reservoirs with suitable recharge conditions and low seepage losses.

The basin in which water is to be stored may be underlain by bedrock or unconsolidated formations of low permeability. It is

8

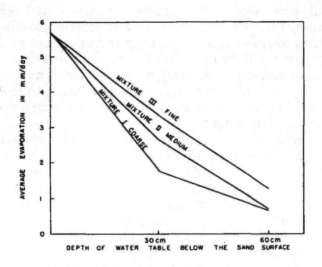

Figure 2.1. Evaporation as a function of depth of water table (Hellwig, 1973).

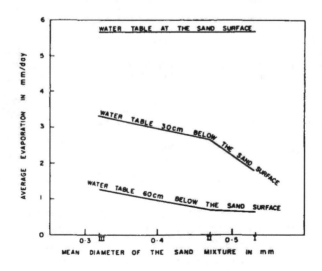

Figure 2.2. Evaporation as a function of grain size (Hellwig, 1973).

generally preferable to site groundwater dams in well-defined and narrow valleys or river beds. This reduces costs and makes it possible to assess storage volumes and to control possible seepage losses. On the other hand storage volumes have to be maximized keeping at the same time dam heights as small as possible. In mountainous areas with very high gradients, it might be difficult to find an acceptable relation between storage volumes and dam height.

The depletion of groundwater storage through natural groundwater flow is the most basic reason for building a sub-surface dam. The gradient of the groundwater table and thus the extent of flow is generally a function of the topographic gradient. This fact indicates that the construction of subsurface dams is feasible only at a certain minimum topographical gradient, which will vary according to local hydrogeological conditions.

Examples of topographical gradients at some construction sites are presented in Table 2.2. Generally the gradient is between 0.2–4 per cent but in extreme cases construction has been made on slopes of 10–16 per cent.

Table 2.2. Topographical gradients at some construction sites.

Site	Type of dam	Gradient (%)
Machakos, Kenya		
general	Sand-storage dam	3-4
extreme	Sand-storage dam	10-15
Bihawana, Tanzania	Sub-surface dam	1.5
Botswana	Sand-storage dam	1
Namibia		
general	Sand-storage dam	0,5-3
extreme	Sand-storage dam	10-15
Shenbagathope, India	Sand-storage dam	0.2
Ottapalam, India	Sub-surface dam	4
Ananganadi, India	Sub-surface dam	3
Ooty, India	Sub-surface dam	16
Arizona, USA	Sand-storage dam	4

The particle size of sediments accumulated along streams and in river beds is generally proportional to the topographical gradient whereas on the other hand, the depth and lateral extent of such deposits is inversely proportional to the gradient. The optimum relation between these two factors, and thus the most favourable sites for sub-surface dams, is generally found on the gentle slopes in the transition zone between hills and plains.

The topography of the impermeable beds or bedrock underlying the storage reservoir determines storage efficiency and methods of dam construction. Figure 2.3 shows how natural underground dams in the form of rock bars improve the natural groundwater conditions (Skibitzke et al., 1961). They may also constitute promising locations for the construction of groundwater dams that would further increase the amount of exploitable water (Sörlie, 1978). Also natural dikes may have a damming effect that could be enhanced by the construction of groundwater dams (Newcomb, 1961). The presence of surface rock bars is generally necessary for the construction of sand-storage dams as is described in the case history from Machakos, Kenya in Chapter 6.

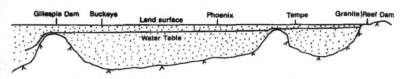

Figure 2.3. Effect of rock bars on ground water table, Salt River Valley, Arizona (from Skibitzke et al., 1961).

An example where optimum topographical conditions prevail is shown in Figure 2.4. An aquifer of even thickness in a wide valley with gentle gradient is drained through a narrow passage between outcropping rock. A dam at this site will create a large amount of storage at comparatively low cost.

3. Hydrogeology
The most favourable aquifers for construction of sub-surface dams are river beds made up of sand or gravel. In-situ-weathered layers and deeper alluvial aquifers have also been dammed with success, even if such aquifers generally have less favourable storage and flow characteristics.

The specific yield of such water-bearing strata may vary from 5 to 50 per cent depending on grain-size distribution, particle shape and compaction (Davis and de Wiest, 1966). Wipplinger (1958) reports a specific yield of approximately

11

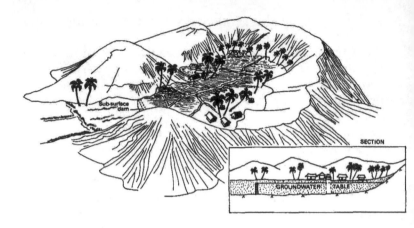

Figure 2.4. Example showing optimum topographical conditions for a sub-surface dam.

25 per cent from a typical river bed in Namibia, whereas the specific yield at the site of a sub-surface dam constructed in a residual-soil aquifer in south India was 7.5 per cent (Ahnfors, 1980). These figures represent fairly well what can be expected in the two types of aquifers.

Hydraulic conductivity values are more sensitive to the type of material constituting the aquifer. The hydraulic conductivity of coarse sand for instance, may be a hundred times higher than that of a very fine sand (Bedinger, 1961) and the presence of clay in a sand aquifer may reduce its hydraulic conductivity thousandfold. The problems that will be encountered when a sub-surface dam is constructed in an aquifer with fine-grained material is thus less related to available storage volumes than to extraction possibilities. The techniques that may be used to solve such problems will be treated briefly in Chapter 5.

A typical profile through a weathered layer is shown schematically in Figure 2.5. According to Taylor (1984) four zones can generally be identified within the profile. The uppermost zones (a) and (b) both have high porosity values but low permeability, whereas zone (c) has low porosity but high permeability. If such an aquifer were dammed, it would provide storage in zones (a) and (b), and zone (c) would act as a natural, and, due to its lateral extent, very effective drain transmitting the water for extraction at the dam wall.

12

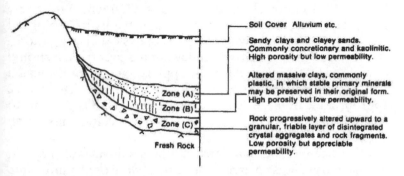

Figure 2.5. Schematic profile of a weathered layer (adapted from Taylor, 1984).

It has been proposed to construct sub-surface dams also in fractured hard-rock aquifers (Larsson and Cederwall, 1980). Such dams would consist of grout curtains cutting off the flow in deep-seated, permeable fracture zones. It would then be possible to stop the drainage effect of such zones and thereby improve the storage in over-lying aquifers. The grout injection technique involved, however, makes this method more suited for large-scale application than for the small-scale rural water supply schemes in developing countries that are within the scope of this text.

Sub-surface dams are, mainly for reasons of the excavation techniques applied, suited for shallow aquifers. The maximum depth of dams in residual soils in south India is 9m. The depth of sub-surface dams built in river beds is generally around 3–6m.

The slope stability of the excavated material, the depth of groundwater at the time of construction and the acceptable costs for any form work that has to be used, set the limit for dam depths.

The fact that aquifers dammed by sub-surface dams are generally shallow means that they are also generally unconfined. Matsuo (1975), however, reports of a sub-surface dam on the island of Kaba in western Japan, which actually dams a confined aquifer at 10–25m depth. Damming at this depth was possible by using injection of bentonite to create a curtain wall in the gravel aquifer. Recharge to the aquifer was increased by an extensive system of sand piles penetrating the confining layer. By damming a deep, confined aquifer it may

13

be possible to control large quantities of water with a relatively small dam area, but it is necessary that the hydrogeological conditions be well known through geophysical investigations. If considered for application in developing countries, it should be realized that it necessitates the application of a sophisticated and expensive technology which might not always be appropriate. For large-scale application where it is possible to accept high construction costs, however, it certainly has a high potential.

The basic idea behind constructing a sub-surface dam for storage purposes is to arrest the natural flow of groundwater, and before it can be judged whether a scheme will be beneficial or not, the extent of flow has to be estimated. The permeability conditions in the aquifers have been treated briefly above. There has rarely been any attempt in the projects studied to quantify the extent of flow by using estimated permeability values and by measuring the actual gradients of the existing groundwater table. In some cases, the seasonal fluctuations of the groundwater levels have been estimated, and this has been used to quantify the additional storage effect resulting from the dam construction. Since any cost-benefit analysis should be based on this figure, it is desirable that efforts are made to make as accurate estimates as possible. This can be done by a fairly simple monitoring programme involving a few observation wells in the aquifer.

Sub-surface dam reservoirs are generally recharged by lateral groundwater flow, and the monitoring programme will give data showing its extent and direction. When the stored water is used for irrigation upstream of the dam, there will also be a substantial recharge from return flow provided the top soils are sufficiently permeable.

Most groundwater dams are founded on solid bedrock. In order to avoid seepage losses below the dam it should be tight, since it is very difficult to stop the leakage through fractures even if they are detected during construction of the dam. Caution should be exercised because the fact that groundwater dams are either constructed in narrow valleys or along rivers, that is along topographical elements that may be considered as indicators of underlying fracture zones.

Under favourable conditions it may also be possible to utilize an existing layer of low permeability as bottom of the storage

14

reservoir. The origin may be alluvial, or it may be the uppermost part of a weathered layer. If sufficiently thick, such layers are generally fairly impermeable but they do not always have the basin structure that is characteristic of the bedrock, and this may cause a lateral loss of water from the reservoir. When groundwater damming is considered for aquifer recharge purposes, however, they may be excellent.

4. Sediments

The accumulation of sediments upstream of a sand-storage dam is the final result of a series of physical processes which will all influence the hydraulic characteristics of the sediments. The parent rock in the catchment is the basis, weathering processes disintegrate the rock, and soil particles are detached by erosion, transported by water and finally deposited in the storage reservoir. Erosion and sedimentation processes in dry climate areas of the world have been studied extensively, mainly in connection with soil conservation activities and the construction of large dams. However, since research has been focused on total rates of erosion in the catchments and on total rates of sediment deposition in the dams, the findings are not directly applicable to our topic, since sand-storage dams utilize only one fraction of the total sediment load.

Hydrological and hydraulic aspects of sedimentation directly relevant to the storage of water in sand-storage dams have been treated extensively by Professor O.Wipplinger. His work is based on studies in Namibia, but the results are probably also applicable to similar parts of the world. The reader is referred to Wipplinger (1958) where detailed studies on river discharge, sediment characteristics in natural river beds and sedimentation processes in pilot sand-storage dam schemes have been excellently presented.

The type of parent rock in the catchment from where sediments originate, determines the amount of coarse particles in the total sediment load. The most favourable rocks are coarse granite, quartzite and sandstone, but dams constructed in gneiss and mica-schist areas have also been successful. Sediments originating from mica-schist areas tend to be more fine grained but the irregular shape increases porosity (Wipplinger, 1958). Areas where the dominating rocks are

15

basalt and rhyolite tend to be less favourable for sand-storage dam construction.

Climate has a great influence on sediment characteristics in that it governs the relation between mechanical and chemical weathering. A lower rate of chemical weathering in arid climates may cause more coarse-grained sediments (Sundborg, 1982).

The total extent of erosion is largely dependent on rainfall intensity, slope and land use. Thus, contrary to what agricultural and hydraulic engineers generally would feel, an engineer planning the construction of a sand-storage dam would be happy to find steep slopes with little vegetative cover in the catchment area.

The coarse sediments one wishes to trap in a sand-storage dam are those generally transported as bedload. It is therefore necessary that the rainstorms producing the initial flows at the onset of the rainy season are sufficiently heavy to cause a bedload transport.

When surveying an area to find out whether it is suitable for the construction of sand-storage dams, one should not be immediately discouraged by the fact that there are no sand deposits along the river. This might be the result of a high-intensity rainfall pattern causing such heavy flows that deposition is not possible under natural conditions. Such conditions prevail, for instance, in parts of Kerala, India (Jacob, 1983).

Chapter 3
USER ASPECTS

1. Water use alternatives

The volumes of water which it is possible to store by groundwater dams of different types and in different physical environments determine the water use. The amounts needed for irrigation purposes are quite large, whereas schemes designed for small-scale drinking water supply may involve the storage of less than 100m^3 and still be economically sound.

Table 3.1 shows how the water stored in some studied schemes is being used.

Table 3.1. Main use of water and approximate volumes stored.

Main water use	Sub-surface dams		Sand-storage dams	
	Number of schemes	Appr. volumes (m^3)	Number of schemes	Appr. volumes (m^3)
Irrigation	9	13,000-10^6	1	6,000
Drinking water (domestic or cattle)	7	400-2,000	9	50-12,000

Generally water stored behind groundwater dams is used for drinking water or irrigation. Only exceptionally is it used also for industrial purposes.

There is a clear functional difference between sub-surface dams and sand-storage dams in terms of water use. Only one of the sand-storage dams is primarily used for irrigation purposes, whereas half of the sub-surface dam schemes supply water for irrigation. The reason for this is clear from the figures of stored volumes. It is possible to store relatively large quantities by damming existing aquifers, and this is generally a pre-requisite when irrigation is considered. It should be mentioned, however, that in some areas of the world a fairly limited quantity of water may help bridge over occasional dry spells during the rainy season or it may prolong the cropping period by a few days thereby making it possible to grow an extra second or third crop.

The way water is used determines which type of water extraction system can be applied. For irrigation schemes it

17

may be economically and technically feasible to construct wells and install motor pumps, whereas for small-scale drinking water supply it may be better to use gravity extraction, or at least make do with hand pumps. The population distribution pattern will also determine the required storage volumes and the choice of extraction and distribution systems.

2. Organizational factors

Most of the schemes planned and executed by government agencies have been executed as pilot projects with the apparent purpose of encouraging imitation. In many areas where such pilot projects have been tried, the effect in terms of new, self-sustained projects has been rather limited. It seems, however, that with the new research and field application programmes mentioned earlier being implemented, there will be a better spreading effect.

In the vicinity of Dodoma in Tanzania a number of sub-surface dams were constructed by the Geological Department and the Public Works Department in the beginning of this century. The available records are incomplete, but at least one of them seems to have been fairly successful. The area is from geographical and technical points of view excellent for the construction of sub-surface dams; the rainfall is scarce and seasonal, the terrain is gentle, thick and well-defined river beds made up of coarse sediments and underlain by low-permeable layers are common features, and dam construction materials are available. In spite of this it took 40 years until one more dam was constructed in 1967, this time on private initiative. The success of this dam proves that groundwater dams are technically feasible in the area, but even so there has up to now been no new attempt. So the reason why the technique is not being used has to be found elsewhere; there is a missing link between the existing technique and its practical application. This is to a large extent an organizational problem and a matter of finding ways to combine efforts from government agencies with the participation of the local users in the planning, construction, operation and maintenance phases. It is also important that the potential users are made aware of the benefits they will get from an improved water supply, for instance by promoting health education. Finally, the knowledge about the technique has to be spread to the geologists and engineers responsible for water supply.

In India the problem has been of a different nature. Two sub-surface dams were built in Kerala State, a part of the country which is densely populated and where the average land holdings are small. Both dams were built on quite large farms; one on a private farm and one on a government seed farm. Since the construction of a dam would generally involve several farms, a more general introduction of the technique in the area depends on the possibilities of promoting co-operative efforts among the farmers. Such efforts are now being made by the State Government under a community irrigation programme. In the neighbouring states of Tamil Nadu and Andhra Pradesh there were earlier isolated examples of groundwater dams. As the knowledge has been developed and experience made available, the techniques now form natural parts of large water conservation and water supply programmes.

Namibia may also serve as an example of where the introduction of the technique has worked well. A successful sand-storage dam was built in 1908 and this example has been followed ever since. The fact that the private farmers in the country can easily realize the economic benefits they derive from increasing the amount of water available for their cattle, has certainly helped.

3. Economic factors
The volumes stored in groundwater dams are usually quite small, and in order to achieve an acceptable cost benefit ratio it is necessary that costs are kept low. The use of expensive investigation methods and construction materials must be avoided, and the participation of expensive technical staff should be limited to a minimum.

The actual costs related to estimated storage volumes are exemplified in Table 3.2.

There are basically two different ways of judging the economic feasibility of using groundwater damming techniques. One is to relate the costs involved directly to the economic benefits accrued from the improved water supply, the other is to compare the cost of a groundwater dam to that of a conventional technical solution. The latter is a rather straightforward method provided some basic data is available,

19

Table 3.2. Cost of stored water in selected schemes

Type of dam	Country	Cost (US$/m³ of estimated storage)	Year of construction	Reference
Sand-storage dam/ concrete	Botswana	2-5	1984	UNESCO, 1984
Sand-storage dam/ concrete	Kenya	1-3	1984	UNESCO, 1984
Sub-surface dam/ brick	India	0.1	1963	Destouni and Johansson, 1987
Sand-storage dam/ concrete and stone masonry	Namibia	0.1	1956-1965	Stengel, 1968

whereas a conventional cost-benefit analysis of water supply for a rural community in a developing country is more difficult to make.

Carruthers and Browne (1977) have described the problems involved in a cost-benefit analysis of water supply projects. Estimating the costs of a project can be done by shadow pricing financial costs and discounting the stream of future costs, even if this involves problems of finding the correct shadow prices and determining an appropriate discount rate. More difficult is to evaluate the future benefits; what are the benefits and how much are they worth in economic terms? When the project supplies water for irrigation it is possible to do this, but if the water is used for domestic purposes, it is not easy to define the benefits economically even if the production and health effects are known and positive. An additional problem is that water supply alone does not improve, for instance, the health conditions in a village; there have to be other inputs like improved sanitation, health education etc. Bearing this in mind, the results of such analyses should be treated with utmost care. One method employed by the World Bank is to use expected revenues as a measure of the benefits, but this is likely to underestimate the real benefits substantially.

Comparing a groundwater dam scheme with a conventional solution is a more simple method. Burger and Beaumont (1970) have compared the cost of a sand-storage dam for drinking water supply to that of a conventional surface reservoir under conditions specific to Namibia. By using depletion charts developed by Wipplinger (1958) they conclude that a conventional dam 12m high and 80m long will yield 20 per cent of the impounded water or 46,000m³ per year, whereas a sand-storage dam of corresponding size will yield 70 per cent of the water stored in the sand or 41,000m3 per year. The similarity of these volume figures is primarily an effect of the evaporation losses involved in surface storage. The construction cost of a sand-storage dam is a bit higher since it has to be constructed over several years with resultant costs of re-establishing the construction gang etc. On the other hand the water in the surface dam has to be purified and the expected useful life of the dam will be limited due to siltation. A cash flow analysis for this example is presented in Table 3.3. The cost of using a sand-storage dam is about 75 per cent of that for a conventional dam under these specific conditions.

Table 3.3. Cash flow analysis for sand-storage and conventional water supply projects (Burger and Beaumont, 1970)

	Year 0	Year 1	Year 2	Year 3	Year 4
1. SAND-STORAGE PROJECT					
(a) Capital expenditure	96,500	60,000	—	21,000	—
(b) Yield in m³/year	391,000	—	—	—	1,000
2. CONVENTIONAL DAM					
(a) Capital expenditure	89,600	95,000	—	—	—
(b) Purification ac/m³	13,200	—	1,740	1,530	1,340
(c) Losses 0.2 c/m³	4,400	—	600	580	540
Total (a), (b) & (c)	107,200	95,000	2,340	2,110	1,880
(d) Yield in m³/year	330,000	—	46,000	43,000	40,000

	Year 5	Year 6	Year 7	Year 8	Year 9
1. SAND-STORAGE PROJECT					
(a) Capital expenditure	18,000	—	—	14,000	—
(b) Yield in m³/year	3,000	6,000	9,000	13,000	20,000
2. CONVENTIONAL DAM					
(a) Capital expenditure	—	—	—	—	—
(b) Purification ac/m³	1,150	1,000	890	770	680
(c) Losses 0.2 c/m³	510	480	440	410	380
Total (a), (b) & (c)	1,660	1,480	1,330	1,180	1,060
(d) Yield in m³/year	36,500	34,000	31,500	29,000	27,000

	Year 10	Year 11	Year 12	Year 13-30	Year 31-
1. SAND-STORAGE PROJECT					
(a) Capital expenditure	—	—	—	—	—
(b) Yield in m³/year	27,000	37,000	41,000	41,000	41,000
2. CONVENTIONAL DAM					
(a) Capital expenditure	—	—	—	—	—
(b) Purification ac/m³	592	514	453	390-0	—
(c) Losses 0.2 c/m³	350	330	300	270-0	—
Total (a), (b) & (c)	942	844	753	660-0	—
(d) Yield in m³/year	25,000	23,000	21,500	19,500-0	—

Cost of water for sand storage project=96,500/391,000=24.7 cent/m3.
Cost of water for conventional dam=107,200/330,000=32.4 cent/m3.
Cost of capital=6 per cent

Chapter 4
PLANNING AND INVESTIGATION METHODS

1. Experience from previous schemes

Most groundwater dam construction schemes are geographically isolated. Very few attempts have been made to make a more thorough regional physical study which would pinpoint areas where the physical conditions would be particularly favourable for different types of dams. Present projects in Ethiopia, India and Brazil are exceptions to this rule (Provisional Military Government of Socialist Ethiopia, 1984; Nilsson, 1987; IPT, 1981 and 1982). Similar projects have been proposed for Israel, Iran and Zimbabwe (Finkel and Finkel, 1978a and b; Bjelm *et al.*, 1986).

There has also generally been a lack of overall physical planning at the local scale, that is within actual project areas. Sites tend to have been chosen quite haphazardly from field trips rather than by systematic studies. There are however positive examples of projects where this is not so, one of them being a sand-storage dam project in Machakos, Kenya.

The Machakos project is also an example of where the construction of groundwater dams has formed a part of an integrated planning effort covering other sectors of societal development. Groundwater dams are useful for water conservation and water supply under certain specific conditions. They are not, however, universally applicable. They should be seen as *alternatives* and their applicability and usefulness should be considered in relation to other activities and conditions in the area under study. Such a holistic approach is being attempted in projects in South India (Nilsson and Sivanappan, 1986; Kandaswamy and Nilsson, 1987). In consequence of the lack of overall planning little use has been made of remote sensing methods like satellite imagery and air-photo interpretation. The geophysical and geotechnical methods applied in some cases have produced only the site-specific data necessary for design, construction and economic analysis.

Since the construction of a groundwater dam generally is a rather straightforward affair which should be cheap, it is understandable that the technical investigation methods used have been simple. The only technical investigations used before the construction of one of the sub-surface dams in South India, for instance, was a steel-rod sounding across the valley to find out the bedrock levels. A more research-oriented scheme in the same area involved land survey, a groundwater level monitoring programme, neutron-probe and tension-plate measurements of specific yield, hammer sounding and geoelectrical measurements.

There are unfortunately many examples of groundwater dams which have not been successful, due to lack of planning and incorrect detailed design. This may have been caused by unforeseen seepage losses through underlying fracture zones, erosion damages due to inappropriate bedrock foundation, etc, or it may have been the result of a total misinterpretation of the groundwater conditions at the site. In some cases it can be concluded that the use of quite simple geophysical methods combined with a proper analysis of the data could have resulted in a better design or the abandonment of an unsuccessful project. There is a need to establish which geophysical methods would be relevant and possibly also to develop new simple investigation aids.

2. Suitable methods

For regional studies the most appropriate instruments are maps of various themes and satellite imagery. Topographical and geological maps are necessary for a regional study, and they generally exist in developing countries even if they may sometimes be difficult to acquire. Also thematic maps showing climatic, hydrological, hydrogeological, soil, vegetation or land-use conditions will yield valuable information. Satellite data is available today in a variety of formats. Digital processing and false-colour techniques are well developed and can be used, but also a plain black-and-white satellite image at a scale of say 1:200,000 is sufficient to draw general conclusions about the geological environment, groundwater conditions, surface runoff and erosion and sedimentation processes.

It is important that reports from previous studies are collected and integrated in the analysis. Such reports will mostly cover the same themes as the maps listed above, but more peripheral subjects may also be of interest. It might, for instance, be possible to find relevant data on erosion and sedimentation in reports issued in connection with irrigation and hydro-power projects.

The local study following a regional analysis that has identified potential implementation areas, will involve more field work and detailed investigations. The best instrument for finding actual groundwater dam sites is air-photo interpretation combined with map studies and field control. Also at this stage it is important to incorporate data from studies carried out previously.

Field measurements of surface water discharge and sedimentation should be made as simple as possible. If gauges are not available it is for instance possible to estimate peak flow levels from marks in the terrain or from interviewing people. Similarly the sediment transport and characteristics can be estimated to some extent from accumulation that has taken place close to existing rock bars.

A proper hydrogeological survey is essential in order to assess the benefits of the construction in terms of increased storage volumes, and in order to get a good general picture of groundwater conditions at the site so that failures can be avoided. Such a study should always involve a water-level monitoring programme covering at least the year before construction. The observation wells which should be placed at suitable distances above and below the dam, can also be used for future evaluation of the functioning of the scheme. If it is not possible to make regular water level observations, useful information can be collected by interviewing local people and by studying water level marks in open wells. When the groundwater level fluctuations are known, it is possible to determine the increased storage of water resulting from the construction of the dam. It also makes it possible to calculate the natural flow of groundwater during different seasons and to assess the amount of groundwater flow that is made accessible for pumping by the dam. The hydrogeological study should also include mechanical sounding or a geoelectrical survey when sub-surface dams are considered. The aquifer material should be hydraulically classified through in-situ as well as laboratory tests. Other hydrogeological methods such as chemical analyses, pumping tests, test drillings etc, should be applied only if necessary and economically feasible.

For economic reasons it is important to limit the use of sophisticated geophysical methods. There are systematic geological methods by which it is possible to use the interpretation of fracture zones in outcropping rocks in the area to predict the potential drainage effect of underlying fracture zones (Larsson, 1984).

The most common construction materials used for groundwater dams are bricks, compacted clay, concrete and stone masonry. The dam has also in general some type of gravel filters for water extraction. To keep construction costs low it is important that as much as possible of the materials used, that is clay, sand, gravel and stones, are available locally. This can be established through a field survey that can run parallel to other field work.

Chapter 5
DESIGN AND CONSTRUCTION

The principle designs of sub-surface dams and sand-storage dams were shown in Chapter 1. Since the two types are basically different, the following presentation of design and construction alternatives has been divided into two parts, followed by a chapter on certain aspects which are common to both types.

1. Sub-surface dams
The storage volumes of some existing schemes were shown in Table 3.1. The actual storage volumes of sub-surface dams range from a few hundred to several million m³ and the designs are consequently quite different. The following presentation concerns mainly small-scale schemes.

(a) Earth work
The most common way of constructing a sub-surface dam is to build a dam in a trench excavated across a valley or a river bed. The earth work involved may be carried out by human labour since the excavation depths are generally not more than 3–6m.

The fact that the material in which the excavation is carried out is generally sandy, creates slope stability problems. Generally a slope of maximum 30° is acceptable for a sandy material and this means that in order to make a 4m deep trench in river sand, the width at ground level would be about 15m. This width can be greatly reduced by using formwork, but this will increase the total costs considerably. Since soil compaction is usually higher at greater depth, however, it is possible to increase the slope gradually. When earth work is carried out by manual labour it is necessary that the excavation is carried out in steps with horizontal levels every 2 or 3m, and this will further increase the width of the excavation.

Sub-surface dams are generally built at the end of the dry season when there is little water in the aquifer. Usually there is some flow, however, and this has to be pumped out during construction.

After the dam has been built the trench is refilled with the excavated material. It is important that the refill is properly compacted by manual compaction and watering. In fact, several failures have been caused by incautious refilling and lack of proper compaction.

(b) Dam construction

Various construction materials have been used for the impermeable screen. Some examples of materials are shown in Figures 5.1–5.8.

The clay dike in Figure 5.1 is an alternative very suitable for small schemes in highly permeable aquifers of limited depth, such as sandy river beds. Clayey top soils are generally available close-by, and they can be mined and transported to the site at low cost. The use of clay is a labour-intensive alternative and there is no need for skilled labour. The clay needs to be properly compacted, and there is a risk of erosion damage to the clay surface due to the groundwater flow. This can be avoided by protecting the dike with plastic sheets. If the storage of groundwater is emptied seasonally, there is a risk that cracks will develop. This can be avoided by making the dike sufficiently thick to retain moisture in the core even during extended dry periods.

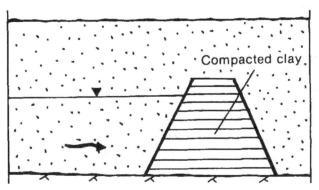

Figure 5.1. Clay dike.

A concrete dam covered on both sides with blocks or stone masonry as shown in Figure 5.2 is an alternative involving rather more advanced engineering for which skilled labour is needed. It necessitates the use of formwork and the availability of cement and gravel. One advantage is that it is possible to raise it above the level of a river bed and use it for further sand accumulation.

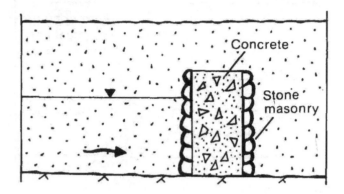

Figure 5.2. Concrete dam.

The same goes for the stone masonry dam shown in Figure 5.3 which is also an alternative necessitating the use of skilled labour and which is suited only for areas where stone masonry work is a part of the engineering tradition, which is not always the case.

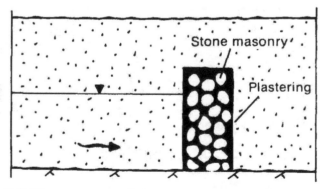

Figure 5.3. Stone masonry dam.

Using ferroconcrete (Figure 5.4) means that steel rods or wire mesh have to be used, but generally such material is available at reasonable cost. The method involves the use of formwork but its main advantage is that very little material is needed to achieve a very strong wall. The structure has to be anchored to a solid reservoir bottom.

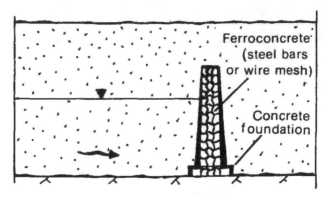

Figure 5.4. Ferroconcrete dam.

Bricks are generally available or may be manufactured from local clay. Building a brick wall as shown in Figure 5.5 and plastering it to make it water tight is a fairly simple procedure. The relatively high cost of bricks is a draw-back, however, and there are also some doubts as to the stability.

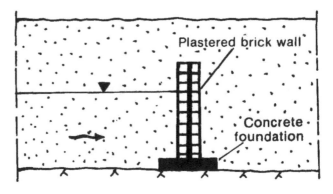

Figure 5.5. Brick wall.

Using thin sheets of impermeable materials such as tarred felt or polyethylene (Figure 5.6) is certainly the least expensive choice as far as material cost is concerned. The mounting of the sheets to wooden frames and the erection process is rather complicated. The material, especially the polyethylene, is highly sensitive to damage during the erection as well as during refilling of the trench, and a minor rip will cause leakage losses. If small sheets are joined together to form the dam, the joints may become weak points that can break due to the water pressure. There are also doubts as to whether plastic material will withstand high groundwater temperatures and the activities of micro-organisms in the soil.

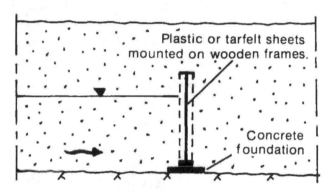

Figure 5.6. Plastic or tarred-felt sheets.

Sheets of steel, corrugated iron or PVC can be used to build up an impermeable wall (Figure 5.7). Even if skilled personnel are needed, for instance for the welding of steel sheets, the construction is quite simple and the result is a sturdy and impermeable structure. One advantage is that the structure can extend over the surface of a river bed and accumulate additional sediments. It is also possible to drive sheets of thick corrugated iron down into river sand from the surface without excavation and without pumping the groundwater. Common sheet piling has been used in connection with the construction of large sub-surface dams in north Africa.

Injection screens (Figure 5.8) have been used to arrest the flow in large or deep-seated aquifers in north Africa and Japan, and to protect fresh water from pollution in Europe and USA. For very large projects and when a deep aquifer is dammed, it is a feasible alternative. One advantage is that the injection can be carried out without having to drain the aquifer.

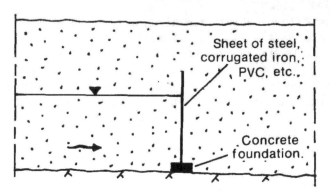

Figure 5.7. Sheets of steel, corrugated iron or PVC.

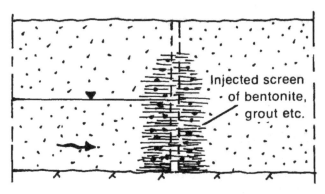

Figure 5.8. Injection screen.

The average heights of some of the dam types are shown in Table 5.1. In most cases the crest of a sub-surface dam is kept at some depth from the surface. This is partly in order to avoid water logging in the upstream area, and partly to avoid erosion damage to the dam. A common distance from dam crest to the surface is about one metre, but it will vary according to local conditions. Water logging can also be avoided if a sluice is incorporated in the dam wall.

(c) Water extraction
A sub-surface dam is usually combined with a drain along the upstream base of the dam. The function of this drain, which generally consists of gravel or a slotted pipe surrounded by a

Table 5.1. Heights of some sub-surface dam types — average values from studied schemes.

Dam type	Average height in metres
Injection screen	10
Brick wall	6
Concrete dam	6
Stone masonry dam	5
Ferroconcrete dam	4
Clay dike	3
Plastic sheets	2

gravel filter, is to collect the water and transmit it to a well or through a gravity pipe to downstream areas. If the permeability of the aquifer material is very low it may be necessary to improve the flow also along the reservoir bottom by a system of collection gravel or slotted-pipe drains perpendicular to the dam. Although this method is more suitable for sand-storage dam reservoirs, it has been applied also in connection with sub-surface damming in river beds.

The well through which water from sub-surface dams is generally extracted may be placed in the reservoir or, for erosion protection reasons, in the river bank. When aquifers with low permeability are dammed it might be necessary to

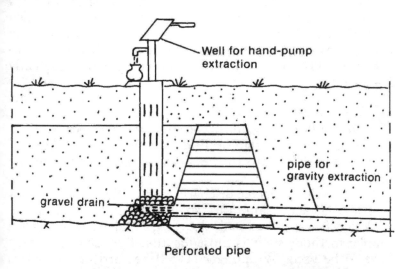

Figure 5.9. Water extraction alternatives from a sub-surface dam.

construct a series of large-diameter wells or collection chambers to create a sufficient storage volume for pumping.

If the community to be served by the scheme is located downstream of the dam site and the topographical conditions are favourable, it is possible to extract water from the reservoir by gravity. By using gravity extraction, problems with pump installation, operation and maintenance are avoided, problems which are today generally encountered in rural water supply projects in developing countries, even in such projects where shallow well and simple hand-pump technology is applied. Figure 5.9 shows a typical sub-surface dam with both extraction alternatives.

2. Sand-storage dams

When a sub-surface dam is built, it is always possible to have at least some idea of the hydraulic characteristics of the existing aquifer material. When planning the construction of a sand-storage dam, however, the material in which the water is to be stored is still lying in the catchment area waiting to be transported to the dam site by a flow of unknown intensity. The proper design of a sand-storage dam is therefore a more complicated matter, involving more hydrological and hydraulic calculations. Wipplinger (1958) has treated the various aspects involved more extensively and some further research has also been indicated in Burger and Beaumont (1970). Design instructions of a very practical nature are given in Nissen-Petersen (1982). The height of a sand-storage dam is typically 1–4 metres.

(a) Water flow

The surface flow of water in the stream under consideration will determine the design of the dam in terms of stability and height, as well as govern the sedimentation process in the reservoir.

An analysis of surface discharge data in the actual river or similar rivers in the same area would make it possible to arrive at design flows. Since such data is generally not available, simpler methods such as those mentioned in Chapter 4 may have to be used. Wipplinger (1958) has arrived at figures representative for Namibia which in turn are based upon experience from the Rocky Mountains in the USA.

The upper limit of dam construction and thus also the upper limit of storage volumes is set by the condition that the dam has to withstand the maximum peak flow which must be discharged safely without causing erosion at the river bank. Proper spillways have to be designed and if necessary, wing walls should be built to protect the banks.

(b) Sedimentation

A sand-storage dam is generally constructed in stages as shown schematically in Figure 5.10.

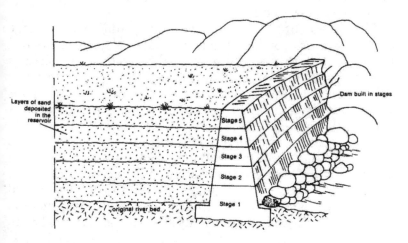

Figure 5.10. Construction principle of sand-storage dam.

The basic idea is to limit the height of each stage in order to keep a sufficiently high velocity of the water so that fine particles are washed out from the reservoir while the coarse particles settle.

The suitable height of each stage can be assessed by studying the extent of natural sedimentation in the stream, or by calculating water velocities in the reservoir. After one stage has been built, the subsequent accumulation of sediments can be studied and the design of the next stage worked out accordingly.

When a large number of dams is constructed within the same project or by the same agency within the same area, the staff will acquire experience which will make it possible to arrive at a suitable stage height only by studying the particular site and by estimating the transport of sediments from the extent of erosion in the area. It is also possible to make quantitative analyses by arriving at limiting flow velocities from studying previous sedimentation.

The settling of fine particles in the reservoir should be avoided as far as possible for several reasons. The specific yield and the permeability of the whole reservoir will be lower, and the evaporation losses higher with a higher percentage of fine particles (Hellwig, 1973). Another factor which is very important is that fine particles in the upper layer will reduce the recharge rates considerably.

The method of constructing the dam by adding a new stage each season or even less frequently means that the costs will be higher than they would be if the dam were constructed to full height directly. Two methods have been tried in order to solve this problem. One is to use a siphon which discharges water over the dam and keeps the flow velocity in the reservoir sufficiently high. This method has been found to be technically inefficient and it is also very costly (Burger and Beaumont, 1970). Another method is to leave a notch in the dam which allows the settling of sediments only up to a certain height. The notch is then filled in before the next rainy season and the reservoir is allowed to be filled completely. This method has proved quite successful in Kenya (Werner and Haze, 1982).

(c) Dam construction
Some dam types are shown in Figures 5.11–5.16.

Figures 5.11 and 5.12 show a concrete and a stone masonry dam respectively. These two types are by far the most common. They fulfil the basic requirement for a sand-storage dam; that is they are sufficiently massive to take up the pressure from the sand and water stored in the reservoir. In addition, they are watertight. For larger reservoirs they may have the form of arch dams.

Figures 5.13 and 5.14 show two examples where the weight of the dam is made up of stone gabions or large blocks which are sufficient to withstand the pressure. In Figure 5.13 the gabion or block dam has been made watertight by covering the upstream side with a thick layer of clay. In Figure 5.14 the core of the dam is made up of a clay wall.

36

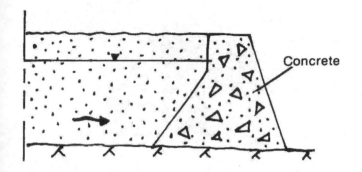

Figure 5.11. Concrete sand-storage dam.

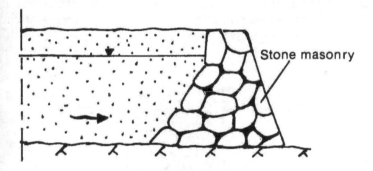

Figure 5.12. Stone masonry sand-storage dam.

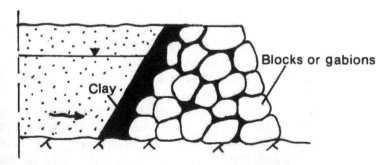

Figure 5.13. Gabion sand-storage dam with clay cover

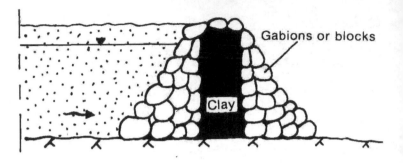

Figure 5.14. Gabion sand-storage dam with clay core.

Figure 5.15 shows an example of a sand-storage dam where the main dam body is made up of a heap of stones which are covered by concrete walls for stability and tightness. There is an example in Kenya where a dam of this type serves at the same time as a bridge over a small stream.

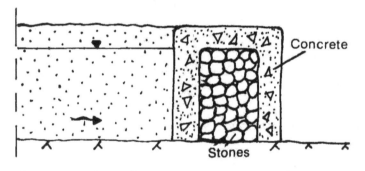

Figure 5.15. Stone-fill concrete sand-storage dam.

A sand-storage dam does not necessarily have to be completely watertight. The dam in Figure 5.16 consists of flat stones which have been piled up to form a massive dam which allows water to seep through it at a rate which is sufficient to water cattle in a trough downstream.

A sand-storage dam has to be well protected against erosion along the banks, and even more so at the dam toe where the energy of water during peak flows will be extremely high. The best way of avoiding erosion is to construct the dam at natural rock bars. If such are not available, the dam should be extended

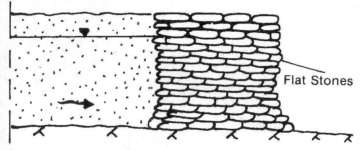
Figure 5.16. Stone sand-storage dam.

several metres into the river bank or complemented with wing walls of sufficient dimensions. The dam should further be protected by an apron at the dam toe.

It is important that sand-storage dams have spillways with sufficient capacity to discharge the overflow during peak flows.

(d) Water extraction

Water extraction alternatives from a sand-storage dam are generally the same as those for a sub-surface dam. Sand-storage dams are even more suitable for gravity extraction than sub-surface dams.

A drain is generally placed at the reservoir bottom along the upstream side of the dam. This drain is connected to a well or a gravity supply pipe through the dam wall. A flushing valve should be installed in the dam to facilitate cleaning of the reservoir if needed.

If it is expected that the accumulated sediments will be fine-grained, it is fairly simple to arrange a system of drains along the reservoir bottom before the sedimentation takes place. As in the case of a sub-surface dam they can be made up by slotted pipes covered by gravel of sufficient grading and quantity to withstand scouring.

If a well is built, it can be made a part of the dam structure. It should be placed at the deepest part of the dam section. If there is a hydraulic connection to the river bank, the well can be protected from scouring by building it in the river bank close to the dam. Figure 5.17 shows an example of such a design from Lubaga River in Tanzania (Wade, 1927).

As mentioned above, one simple extraction alternative is to allow a seepage through the dam which can then be collected

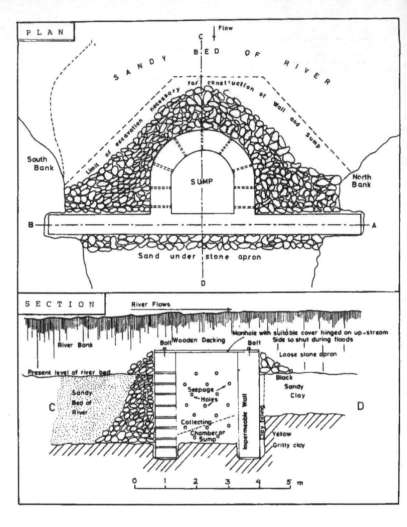

Figure 5.17. Plan and section of proposed dam in Lubaga River, Tanzania (Wade, 1927).

immediately at the downstream side or in a well or trough at some distance along the course of the stream.

A typical sand-storage dam with extraction alternatives is shown in Figure 5.18.

40

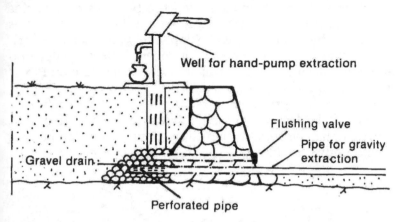

Figure 5.18. Extraction alternatives from a sand-storage dam.

3. Common Aspects
(a) Bedrock foundation
Groundwater dams should as far as possible be anchored in solid rock. This generally gives the best stability and it makes it possible in most cases to control seepage below the dam. Anchoring may be done by a concrete foundation on the rock surface. If the rock is weathered, the weathered profile should be fully excavated before the dam foundation is made, otherwise there is a risk of seepage below the dam.

When fresh rock is encountered after excavation, it should be checked for possible open fracture zones. The rock surface should be cleaned properly and simple infiltration tests carried out if it is suspected that there might be fractures. If a leakage is established it might be possible to stop it by pressure grouting or by pouring very thin mortar into the fracture zone after it has been excavated as deep as possible. It is important, however, that the full length of the zone is checked out and sealed off if necessary. If it is not possible to stop the leakage and if it is not feasible to use the fracture as a natural extraction alternative, the implementation of the scheme may have to be reconsidered.

(b) Replenishment of natural aquifers
A groundwater dam may function as a recharging structure for an already existing aquifer by lateral or vertical flow.

Figure 5.19 shows an example from Namibia of how this can work (Sauermann, date unknown). A dike was utilized as an aquifer by means of a well supplying water to an airport. The aquifer did not carry enough water to meet the demand and it was decided to construct a sand-storage dam on top of it, thereby increasing the recharge.

Sometimes a groundwater dam is considered a failure because it is drained out by a fracture system. It might, however, then be possible to drill a well in the zone and utilize the groundwater dam as an artificial recharge structure.

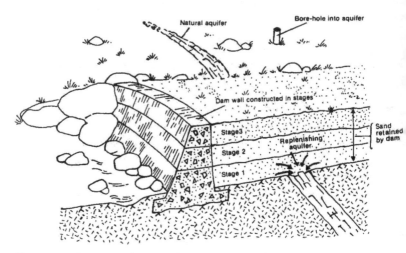

Figure 5.19. Groundwater dam for recharging purposes (from Sauermann, date unknown).

(c) Recharge
When sub-surface dams are constructed in areas where the top soil layers have low permeability or where gradients are high, it might be necessary to improve the recharge to the reservoir by surface flow diversion, trench or pit digging etc. This can be done also for sand-storage dams where the upper layers have been silted, and where it is not feasible to remove the silt mechanically.

(d) Series of dams
In some areas it might be possible to construct a whole series of interconnected ground water dams. Such potentials have

been identified along sandy river beds in Kenya (Sørlie, 1978) and along narrow and very long valleys in South India (Nilsson, 1987; Anjaneyulu, 1985). The 'jessours' of Tunisia are examples of small-scale dams that may be placed at regular intervals along alluvial valleys (El Amani, 1979). In the specific example shown in Figure 5.20 it was possible to determine the rate of siltation by comparing the level of a 50-year-old weir with the present level.

Figure 5.20. Jessour, Tunisia (from El Amani, 1979).

(e) Environmental impact

If planned and executed properly, a scheme involving damming of groundwater should have no direct negative impact on the surrounding environment. It should be kept in mind, however, that the technique is implemented in a fragile environment where even a small change may have long-term physical as well as social consequences. This calls for caution in the planning of schemes.

The fact that the natural water flow is arrested means that there may be an effect on the groundwater conditions in downstream areas. Such possible effects must be considered during the planning of schemes.

43

There is a risk of water logging of upstream areas. This problem can be solved by keeping the crest of sub-surface dams well below ground level or by having a sluice in the dam. In the case of sand-storage dams this will not be a big problem because there is generally no effective land use in the area that may be influenced.

The fact that groundwater levels will rise means that the risk of pollution increases. When the water is used for drinking purposes it may be necessary in some cases to protect the recharge areas by fencing or by soil or vegetative cover.

The water stored behind sub-surface dams may be used for irrigation in the area above the dam. In this way the return seepage is collected in the reservoir and may be used again. This re-circulation is certainly a good way of conserving water, but it may create problems with salt accumulation if the seasonal rains are not sufficiently heavy to wash out the salts accumulated in the soil. There may also be some salinization of soil and groundwater caused by evaporation if the groundwater level is shallow.

Chapter 6
CASE HISTORIES

The reader is referred to the map in Figure 1.3 where areas with known groundwater dam schemes are shown. In the following a resumé of the activities in these areas is made, and more detailed descriptions are given from three selected areas in Kenya, Tanzania and India.

1. Europe
Groundwater dams built by the Romans still exist on Sardinia (Tröften, 1982), and several schemes in Germany, France and Italy where sub-surface dams have been used mostly to raise groundwater levels are presented in Gignoux and Barbier (1955), Guembel (1945 and 1947) and BCEOM (1978). Sand-storage dams primarily serving as stream-flow moderators, have been constructed in mountainous regions of Austria (Baurne, 1984). Sub-surface dams serving the purpose of containing water in existing aquifers have been constructed in Greece (Garagunis, 1981) and sub-surface dams mainly functioning as protection against sea-water intrusion into fresh-water aquifers have been proposed in Yugoslavia (Pavlin, 1973) and Greece (Garagunis, 1981). There is a proposal for a large sub-surface dam in Sicily, that would supply 73 million m^3 per year (Aureli, 1983).

2. Africa
Several very large sub-surface dam schemes primarily designed to increase the groundwater availability for irrigation purposes exist in north-western Africa, notably in Morocco and Algeria (Robaux, 1954; Duquesnoy, date unknown; BCEOM, 1978), and have been proposed for construction in Mauritania (Guiraud, 1980). In Tunisia the 'jessours' represent a special type of sand-storage dam which is very slowly filled with sediments and at the same time used for growing olive trees (El Amani, 1979). Sub-surface dams have been built in Cape Verde Islands and Botswana (UNESCO, 1984).

In the Hararghe Region of Ethiopia, a number of sub-surface dams for drinking water supply have been constructed in river beds during the last few years and several are proposed for construction within the near future (Hansson and Nilsson, 1986; Provisional Military Government of Socialist Ethiopia, 1984). A large sub-surface dam scheme involving jet injection has been proposed in Nogal District, Somalia (Pozzi and Benvenuti, 1979).

Groundwater dams are quite frequently used for water supply in East Africa. Examples of sand-storage dams in Machakos Region, Kenya, and sub-surface dams close to Dodoma, Tanzania, are presented in detail below. Sub-surface dams in river beds are quite frequent in the area east of Nairobi and have been proposed for construction in North Turkana (Sørlie, 1978). In Tanzania the known schemes are concentrated around Dodoma, but some are also reported from the southern parts of the country (Mitchell, 1954), and one close to Lake Victoria in the north (Wade, 1927).

There is a mention of sub-surface dams in Zambia (Verboom, date unknown). The potential of using groundwater dams in northern Mozambique has been reported by de Sonneville (1982) and Ferro (1982), and in Zimbabwe by Dahlin *et al.*, 1984.

Increasing the water available for domestic supply and for watering of cattle by means of building sand-storage dams is a widely adopted technique in arid parts of Namibia. Numerous examples exist and have been described by Wipplinger (1958, 1961, 1965, 1974, 1982, 1984a and undated), Aubroeck (1971), Burger and Beaumont (1970), Beaumont and Kluger (1973), Stengel (1968) and Sauermann (date unknown). There are also some sub-surface dams (Wipplinger, 1984b).

(a) Machakos, Kenya

The climate in the Machakos area is semi-arid with an average, and highly seasonal, rainfall of about 850 mm/year, and a potential evaporation of about 1.600–1.800 mm/year. The bedrock is mostly Pre-Cambrian and the topography is hilly.

Old sub-surface dams in river beds and sand-storage dams in gullies are quite common in the area. One such old dam is shown in Figure 6.1. The dam was built in 1961 but without extending the abutments properly into the river banks. Sediments have been trapped upstream of the dam, but due to erosion the river has taken a new course around the dam, thus making the dam useless for water storage purposes.

Figure 6.1. Old eroded sand-storage dam, Machakos.

A large number of sand-storage dams have been built under the Machakos Integrated Development Programme (Werner and Haze, 1982). The siting of the dams as well as the estimation of erosion and sediment transport was made mainly by using air-photo interpretation with subsequent field checks.

The basic criteria used for a dam site were the availability of rock bars and the existence of natural basins for sand accumulation. All dams were of gravity type and built of stone masonry.

Figures 6.2 and 6.3 show a dam built in Mukio. The dam is built on top of an already existing 'bridge' across a river. The additional height is about 2m. The area above the dam is almost completely filled up with sand. The dam is constructed in three parts: two dam walls of about 50cm width surrounding a fill of stones covered by a cement layer constituting the road surface. It took 10 months to construct the dam.

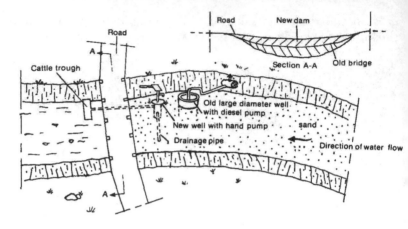

Figure 6.2. Plan and section of Mukio sand-storage dam site, Machakos.

Figure 6.3. Mukio sand-storage dam, Machakos.

Figures 6.4 and 6.5 show a sand-storage dam built in Kyandili. This quite large dam was built using the V-notch method. Instead of building the dam in sections each year, the whole dam was built on one occasion but a notch was left in

48

the centre to allow silt outflow. After one season of sand accumulation the notch was closed and the dam was then completely filled with sand after the next rains. The notch can be seen in Figure 6.6.

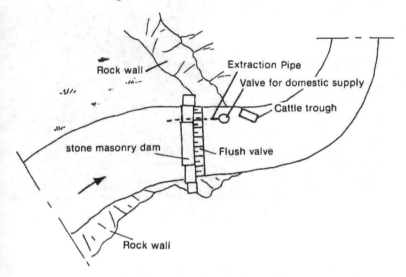

Figure 6.4. Plan of Kyandili sand-storage dam site, Machakos.

Figure 6.5. Kyandili sand-storage dam, Machakos.

Figure 6.6. Filled-in notch, Kyandili sand-storage dam, Machakos.

The dam height is about 3m and the total cost of construction was 35,000 Kenyan shillings. It was supplied with a pipe outlet and valve. At the bottom of the dam there is a pipe for flushing the reservoir.

A special type of sand-storage dam is shown in Figures 6.7 and 6.8. The idea behind this scheme is to store the water in the main surface dam but let water for drinking purposes in a pipe down to a sand-storage dam where it is extracted from a well equipped with a hand pump.

It was estimated that the sediments carried in the small tributary to the main stream would be enough to fill the dam. The drainage area of the tributary is about 1.5km². The purpose of this sand-storage dam is thus to serve as a slow sand filter and not to store water. The flow to the sand-storage dam will be automatically regulated by a ball valve. The sand-storage volume is estimated at about 150m³.

A general impression of the sand-storage dam project in Machakos is that the schemes have been quite successful. The few problems encountered relate to operation and maintenance of the schemes, but they seem to be less than for water supply projects of conventional types.

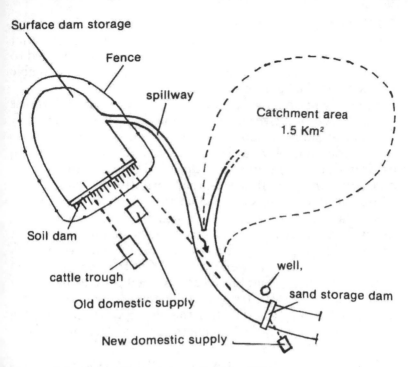

Figure 6.7. Plan of Kalusi dam site, Machakos.

Figure 6.8. Kalusi sand-storage dam, Machakos, before sedimentation.

(b) Dodoma, Tanzania

The earliest reference to a sub-surface dam in Tanzania is that of a dam built in 1912 near Dodoma. The dam is referred to very briefly in Fawley (1956), but there are no records available on the type of construction or the exact location.

In 1927 a masonry wall with a concrete core was built across the sand bed of a river near Dodoma (Tanganyika Territory Geological Survey Annual Report, 1928). The objective was to provide water for cattle as well as human consumption during the dry period. No detailed description of the construction is available, but apparently the dam was a combination of a sub-surface dam and a dam projecting over the surface with the purpose of trapping sediments during heavy flows. This latter objective was fulfilled during the rains of late 1927 when the dam was completely filled with sand. Unfortunately the rains were so heavy that they also destroyed some of the piping that had been installed for conveyance of stored water to a cattle trough on the down-stream side. Some alterations aiming at protecting the piping were made during 1928 and apparently the scheme then functioned properly, at least during the rains of 1928.

It was calculated that the total effective storage volume behind the dam would be $410m^3$ which would provide for a daily supply of $2.3m^3$ during the dry season. During 1928, which was apparently an abnormally dry year, stock were watered for two months of the dry period until grazing in the vicinity of the dam was exhausted. Calves and small stock were watered throughout the dry period.

In 1928 another sub-surface water conservation scheme was constructed at a place called Kikuyu. The scheme involved the construction of some type of sub-surface dam, but there are no construction details available. Since the objective was to supply water for town, stock and railway requirements, it was probably quite a large scheme. It functioned quite well during the year of 1928 when it supplied water for the railway requirements. This was in spite of failure of the rains and the fact that some $27,000m^3$ of water had to be pumped to waste for drainage purposes during construction.

A more recent scheme was constructed at Bihawana about 15km south-west of Dodoma. The river in which the dam was built is intermittent and flows to the west about 500m north of the Bihawana Roman Catholic Mission which is situated on a high hill (Figure 6.9). The river bed consists of coarse sand and has a width of about 20m. The banks rise 1m above the sand level and are covered by dense bush vegetation. Women traditionally collect water from holes dug in the sand above the dam site.

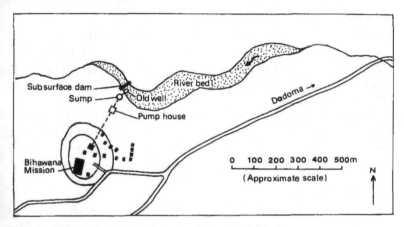

Figure 6.9. Plan of Bihawana scheme, Dodoma.

In the early fifties the fathers of the mission constructed a well in the river bed. It has a diameter of about 3m and has concrete lining and top cover. This well was used for supply to the mission until the mid sixties when it was no longer sufficient for a safe supply during the dry season.

In 1967 a dam was constructed in order to trap water upstream which would be sufficient for water supply throughout the year. A trench was dug across the river down to a layer of calcrete, or the upper part of the weathered rock. This layer was encountered at about 3m depth. The excavation was done by manual labour only. A clay dike was built in the trench. The clay was brought in by truck from somewhere in the vicinity of Bihawana. On the upper side of the dam a gravel pack was constructed and inside this a slotted collector pipe of 18cm diameter was placed at the bottom of the dam. This pipe collects the water which flows by gravity to a sump of 6m depth constructed in the river bank. The sump is connected to a pump house from where the water is pumped to the mission. A pipe also connects the old well to the sump.

The system has been working since the year of construction and today supplies water to some 25 people, 100 pigs and for irrigation of a vegetable garden of one quarter of an acre. The sump never dries out but maintains a level of about 1–1.5m above the bottom even at the end of the dry season (Kifua, 1981).

3. Asia

Large-scale sub-surface dam projects have been proposed in western Saudi Arabia by Basmaci (1983). The construction of a relatively small sub-surface structure damming an extensive aquifer in Charuli, Afghanistan, has been reported by Guembel (1945 and 1947).

Sub-surface dams have been proposed for construction in Thailand and at several sites in Japan by Matsuo (1975 and 1977), who also reports of a sub-surface dam constructed by means of jet injection on the island of Kaba in western Japan.

(a) South India

The following account is based on Ahnfors (1980), Basak *et al.*, (1985), Destouni and Johansson (1987), Hanumantha Rao (1985), Kandaswamy and Nilsson (1987), Kittu (1979), Nilsson (1983b, 1984 and 1985), Nilsson and Sivanappan (1985 and 1986), Raju (1983) and *The Hindu* (1986 and 1987).

Two sub-surface dams have been constructed in Kerala, South India. The sites are situated in the Palghat Gap which is a graben dividing two hill ranges parallel to the west coast. The altitude is about 50m and rainfall averages 2,400mm, the main part of which comes in June-October.

Agriculture is intensive in the area. The water available during the rainy season is enough to grow one rice crop, and in part of the area two crops in a year. There is a need for additional water to expand the area covered by a second crop, and also to irrigate a third crop.

One factor restricting the possibility of constructing groundwater dams in this area is that land holdings are generally small, and it is difficult to organize the co-operative effort needed when several farmers are involved. Thus, the two existing dams are both situated on quite large farms. One was constructed by a private farmer and the other was built on a government seed farm by the Central Ground Water Board of India.

The private dam was constructed in Ottapalam in 1962–64. A large-diameter well supplying water to the farm usually dried out during the dry season and there was a need to find an alternative solution. A 155m long dam reaching down to bedrock was built across a narrow valley, surrounded by out-cropping rocks (Figure 6.10).

Figure 6.10. Sub-surface dam at Ottapalam, Kerala.

Figure 6.11. Brick wall of Ottapalam sub-surface dam, Kerala.

The depth to freshrock, which was established prior t
excavation by steel-rod sounding, is on average 5m and reache
a maximum of 9m at the centre of the valley. The aquife
consists of residual soils which, at least in the upper layer:
are sandy. The transition between the weathered layer and th
underlying fresh rock is distinct, and it was established durin
the excavation that the rock had no major fracture zones.

The dam consists of a 4-inch plastered brick wall (Figur
6.11). Water is extracted from the aquifer through a grave

drain along the dam, to a series of collector wells feeding a pumping well. The dam has been supplied with a sluice in one of the collector wells. By this arrangement it is possible to regulate the groundwater level in the reservoir and avoid water logging in the fields above the dike. The catchment area of the dam is about 10ha and water is used for irrigation of 3.2ha of paddy during October-December, and 1.2 ha of paddy during the dry season.

Figure 6.12. Excavation of trench at Ananganadi, Kerala. (Photo: E.Danfors).

The dam built by the Central Ground Water Board was completed in 1979. In addition to supplying water for supplementary irrigation at the seed farm it was also meant to serve as a pilot project for future dam construction. In consequence, a more scientific approach was used at the hydrogeological investigations.

This dam was also constructed across a narrow valley and has a catchment area of about 20ha. The bedrock consists of gneiss and granite which crops out on the valley sides. The in-situ weathered soils are sandy in the central parts of the valley and more fine-grained along the sides. The average specific yield determined from tension-plate and neutron-probe measurements is 7.5 per cent. Other investigations carried out at the site were hammer soundings and resistivity measurements to establish the depth to bedrock which at the deepest section is about 5m. The excavation of the trench is shown in Figure 6.12.

The total length of the dam is about 160m and the crest was kept 1m below ground level in order to avoid water logging in the up-stream area. The main part of the dam is made up of a plastered brick wall but there are also sections consisting of tarred felt and plastic sheets (Figure 6.13). Two wells, connected to each other by drill holes through a rock bar, were constructed along the dike (Figure 6.14).

The dam took three months to complete at a total cost of 7,500 dollars, including pumping equipment. One third of this cost was for earth work and the rest for equipment and construction materials. The storage volume of the reservoir was estimated at 15,000m^3. A recent study has shown that water leaks out from the reservoir through a crack in the brick wall at the place of one of the wells and through the tarred felt sections. Thus the capacity of the scheme has been greatly reduced.

A sub-surface dam was built in Ootacamund, Tamil Nadu, in 1981. The dam, made of plastic sheets, was built in a weathered layer and supplies water for irrigation. The sheets are 2m deep and extend down into a layer of clay. A surface earth dam of about 1.5m height has been built on top of the sub-surface dam. The function of the scheme is that the sub-surface dam collects the groundwater flow on top of the clay layer and diverts it to the surface, where it is stored behind the surface dam (Figure 6.15).

Figure 6.13. Mounting of tarred felt sheets, Ananganadi, Kerala. (Photo: O.Ahnfors).

Figure 6.14. Site of sub-surface dam at Ananganadi, Kerala.

Figure 6.15. Site of the combined surface/sub-surface dam at Ootacamund, Tamil Nadu.

A combined sub-surface/sand-storage dam was built by the Forest Department at Shenbagathope, Tamil Nadu, in 198. A stone masonry dam extends to 3.5m depth in a sandy river bed of about 15m width. The crest of the dam is 0.75m above the present sand level and there is provision to raise it further as sand accumulates above the dam. The dam is intended to improve the supply of water to the nearby town of Srivilliputtur.

Groundwater dams form part of large water conservation projects presently being taken up by the Tamil Nadu Forest Department. They are also included in several research and drought relief programmes in Kerala and Tamil Nadu.

Several sub-surface dams have been built by the Minor Irrigation Department in sandy river beds in Andhra Pradesh.

The 'anicuts' of the large rivers in Tamil Nadu are basically irrigation water diversion structures, but are extended to some depth below surface, thus causing a substantial rise of groundwater levels which benefits nearby wells.

4. America

There is a long tradition of building groundwater dams in the arid south-western parts of the United States and northern Mexico. Sub-surface dams called 'tapoons' have been constructed in sandy river beds in Arizona (Lowdermilk, 1953), and sand-storage dams have been built in semi-desert regions of Arizona and Sonora, the oldest one already in the eighteenth century (Sykes, 1937). A large sub-surface dam was built across Pacoima Creek, California in 1887–1890. The dam has a length of 200m and a maximum depth of 17m and consists of a 0.6m thick masonry wall (Schuyler, 1896; Slichter, 1902; Dixey, 1931). Helweg and Smith (1978) report a type of artificial aquifer built in New Mexico and elsewhere, which involves a small basin being excavated, covered with PVC or clay and then refilled with sand. The excavated material is used for a dam which retains water in the reservoir. A similar artificial aquifer of larger size is used for stormwater retention in Akron, Ohio (The American City, 1974). Grouted sub-surface dams have been proposed for the City of Newark, Delaware (Willis, date unknown).

The suitability of groundwater dams for rural water supply in the dry Nordeste Region of Brazil has been established by Pompeu dos Santos & Frangipani (1978), Leite and Oliveira (1982), Oliveira and Leite (1984), Veja (1984) and IPT (1981), and there are also examples of old dams in that region (Dixey,

1931; IPT, 1981). Four sub-surface dams were built by IPT in 1982 (IPT, 1982).

Small-scale sub-surface dams were built in river beds in Bolivia in 1983 under a drought relief project supported by Swedish Emergency Aid (World Water, 1984).

LIST OF REFERENCES

Ahnfors, O., 1980. 'Groundwater arresting sub-surface structures'. Govt. of India, *SIDA-assisted Ground-Water Project in Noyil, Ponnan and Amaravati River Basins, Tamil Nadu and Kerala,* Report 1:16, 22 p.

Anjaneyulu, D., 1985. *Report on aerial photo study of Kole Lands and its environs, Trichur District, Kerala State.* Central Ground Water Board, Coastal Kerala Ground Water Project, Report 4. Trivandrum, 15 pp.

Aubroeck, L., 1971. 'Sand dams could save dry areas from destruction'. *Farmer's Weekly,* August 25, 1971. South-West Africa, pp. 4–8.

Aureli, A., 1983. 'L'usage conjoint superficielles et d'eauxsouterraines dans un bassin ou l'on a un grand aquifere constitute de roches volcaniques'. *Proc. International Symposium on Groundwater in Water Resources Planning, Koblenz.* IAHS Publication No. 142, pp. 675–683.

Basak, P.; Rajagopalan, S.P.; Nazimuddin, M.; Narasimha Prasad, N.B.; Nilsson, A., 1985. *Storage of groundwater in the valley fills of western Ghats for rural water supply—A project proposal.* Centre for Water Resources Development and Management, Kozhikode. 20 pp.

Basmaci, Y., 1983. 'Underground dams for ground-water development'. Summary of paper to be presented at the Groundwater Technology Division's Education Section, International Water Well Exposition, St Louis, USA, Sept. 13–14, 1983. Groundwater, 21:4, p. 522.

Baurne, G., 1984. 'Trap-dams: artificial sub-surface storage of water'. *Water International,* Vol.9, No.1, pp. 2–9.

Beaumont, R.D.; Kluger, J.W., 1973. 'Sedimentation in reservoirs as a means of water conservation'. *IAHR Congress,* Istanbul, 3–7 September 1973, pp. A28–1-A28–6.

Bedinger, M.S., 1961. 'Relation between median grain size and permeability in the Arkansas River Valley, Arkansas'. *US Geol. Survey Prof. Paper 424-C,* pp. 31–32.

Bjelm, L.; Rapp, A.; Dahlin, T.; Håsteen, C., 1986. *Groundwaterdams in southern Zimbabwe—Proposed research.* Lund University of Science and Technology. 23 pp.

Bureau Central d'Etudes pour les Equipements d'Outre-Mer

(BCEOM), 1978. 'Les barrages souterrains'. Ministère de la Coopération. 135 pp.

Burger, S.W.; Beaumont, R.D., 1970. 'Sand storage dams for water conservation'. *Convention: water for the future. Water Year 1970.* Republic of South Africa, 9 pp.

Carruthers, I.; Browne, D., 1977. The economics of community water supply'. In: *Water, Wastes and Health in Hot Climates* (eds. Feachem, R.; McGarry, M.; Mara, D.). John Wiley & Sons. 399 pp.

Central Ground Water Board, 1980. *SIDA-Assisted Groundwater project in Noyil, Ponnani, and Amaravati River Basins, Tamil Nadu and Kerala; Project Findings and Recommendations.* Government of India. 48 pp.

Dahlin, T.; Hallberg, M.; Håsteen, C., 1984. *The water situation around Chabwira, Mberengwa District. Midlands Province, Zimbabwe.* University of Lund, LUTVDG/TVTG-5010/1-/1984. 80pp.

Davis, S.N.; De Wiest, R.J.M., 1966. *Hydrogeology.* John Wiley & Sons. 463 pp.

de Sonneville, J., 1981. National Directorate of Water, Mozambique. Personal communication.

Destouni, G.; Johansson, M., 1987. *Seasonal storage of groundwater— A study of groundwater dams in South India.* The Royal Institute of Technology, Hydraulics Laboratory, Examensarbete No.312, Stockholm. 29 pp.

Dixey, F., 1931. *A practical handbook of water supply.* Thomas Murby & Co., London.

Duquesnoy, C., date unknown. *Barrage de Tadjemout.* Terres et Eaux, No.5. 21 pp.

El Amani, S., 1979. Traditional technologies and development of the African environments; utilization of runoff waters, the "meskats" and other techniques in Tunisia'. *African Environment,* Vol.111, 3–4, No.11–12, pp. 107–120.

Fawley, A.P., 1956. 'Water resources of Dodoma and vicinity'. *Rec. Geol. Survey Tanganyika.,* Vol.111, pp. 62–70.

Fellows, J.; Fridfeldt, A., 1982. 'Koma rock—a study of an inselberg in the North Machakos-Thika area, Kenya'. In: *Geomorphological studies in Central Kenya, report from a field course, March, 1982* (eds Lundén, B.; Strömquist, L.). Depts. of Physical Geography of Stockholm, Uppsala, Lund.

Ferro, B.P.d.A., 1982. GEOMOC, Mozambique. Personal communication.

Finkel & Finkel Ltd., 1978a. *Underground dams in arid zone riverbeds.* Haifa, Israel. 7 pp.

Finkel & Finkel Ltd., 1978b. *Underground water storage in Iran—reconnaisance survey.* Haifa. 16 pp.

Garagunis, C.N.,1981. 'Construction of an impervious diaphragm for improvement of a sub-surface water-reservoir and simultaneous protection from migrating salt water'. *Bulletin of the International Association of Engineering Geology,* No.24, pp. 169–172.

Gignoux, M.; Barbier, R., 1955. 'Barrages souterrains dans les alluvions'. In: *Géologie des barrages et des aménagement hydraulique,* p. 262. Paris.

Guembel, W., 1945. 'Apercu sur la construction des barrages souterrains'. *Institut Techn. du Batiment et des Travaux Publics,* Circulaire Série K., No. 12, 4 pp.

Guembel, W., 1947. 'Barrages et retenues souterraines'. *La Technique Sanitaire et Municipale,* Septembre-Octobre, 1947. pp. 70–75.

Guiraud, R., 1980. *Projet de gestion des ressources en eau dans la region du Brakna Oriental et de l'Aftout.* Ministère du Développement Rural/Direction de l'Hydraulique. 24 pp.

Hansson, G.; Nilsson, Å., 1986. 'Groundwater dams for rural water supplies in developing countries'. *Ground Water,* Vol.24, No.4, July-August 1986, pp. 497–506.

Hanumantha Rao, T., 1985. 'Groundwater for large scale irrigation development in Rayalaseema'. Unpublished paper. Hyderabad. 3 pp.

Hellwig, D.H.R., 1973. 'Evaporation of water from sand, 4: The influence of the depth of the water-table and the particle size distribution of the sand'. *Journal of Hydrology,* 18 (1973) 317–327.

Helweg, O.J.; Smith, G., 1978. 'Appropriate technology for artificial aquifers'. *Ground Water,* Vol.16, No.3, May-June 1978, pp. 144–148.

Instituto de Pesquisas Technológicas do Estado de São Paulo (IPT), 1982. 'Estudos, projetos e costruçao de barragens subterrâneas nos rios das Cobras e dos Quinos—Bacia do rio Seridó—Municipios de Parelhas e Equador—Rio Grande do Norte'. *Relatório No. 17 023, IPT, Minas e Geologia Aplicada.* São Paulo. 43 pp.

Instituto de Pesquisas Technológicas do Estado de São Paulo (IPT), 1981. 'Levantamento das potencialidades para implantacao de barragens subterrâneas no Nordeste brasileiro—Bacias dos rios Piranhas-Acu (RN) e Jaguaribe (CE)'. *Relatório No. 14 887.* 56 pp.

Jacob, V.C., 1983. *Central Ground Water Board, India. Personal communication.*

Kandaswamy, P.; Nilsson, Å., 1987. *Water harvesting in Western Ghats, India—Background document for discussions in Stockholm.* May 1987. 8 pp.

Kifua, G., 1981. Ministry of Water and Energy, Tanzania. Personal communication.

Kittu, N., 1979. 'Occurrence groundwater in hard rocks and criteria for design and construction of wells in Kerala State'. *International Seminar on Development and Management of Groundwater Resources,* November 5–20, 1979, University of Roorkee, India.

Larsson, I., 1984. 'Hydrological significance of fractures'. In: *Ground Water in Hard Rocks,* IHP Report No.33, UNESCO, Paris.

Larsson, I.; Cederwall, K., 1980. 'Underground storage of water in natural and artificial openings in hard rocks in developing countries'. *Rockstore 80, International Symposium for Environmental Protection, Low-Cost Storage and Energy Savings,* Stockholm, June 23–27, 1980. 6 pp.

Leite, C.A.G.; Oliveira, A.M.S., 1982. 'Viabilidade de implantaçao de barragens subterràneas no semi-árido'. *1 Simpósio Brasileiro do Trópico Semi-Arido,* agosto, 1982. 21 pp.

Lowdermilk, W.C., 1953. 'Some problems of hydrology and geology in artificial recharge of underground aquifers'. In: *Ankara Symposium on Arid Zone Hydrology Proceedings,* UNESCO, pp. 158–161.

Matsuo, S., 1975. 'Underground dams for control groundwater'. *Publication No. 117 de l'Association Internationale des Sciences Hydrologiques,* Symposium de Tokyo (Décembre, 1975).

Matsuo, S., 1977. 'Environmental control with underground dams'. *Proceedings of the Speciality Session on Geotechnical Engineering and Environmental Control. Ninth International Conference on Soil Mechanics and Foundation Engineering,* Tokyo, July 1977. pp. 169–182.

Mitchell, T., 1954. 'Water conservation in southern Tanganyika'. *Corona,* Vol.6, p. 414.

Newcomb, R.C., 1961. 'Storage of ground water behind sub-surface dams in the Columbia River basalt, Washington, Oregon, and Idaho'. US Geol. Survey Prof. Paper 383-A, pp. A1-A15.

Nilsson, Å., 1983. 'Siting of ground-water dams—hydrogeological and planning aspects. Proposed research in Kerala'. Unpublished research programme, Department of Land Improvement and Drainage, Royal Institute of Technology, Stockholm.

Nilsson, Å., 1984. 'Conservation and development of groundwater by means of groundwater dams'. Unpublished paper presented at meeting in Tunis, October 1984. 11 pp.

Nilsson, Å., 1985. 'Siting of groundwater dams for rural water supply in developing countries—hydrogeological and planning aspects'.

Proceedings of the Fifth World Congress on Water Resources, Vol.3, pp.1287–1296.

Nilsson, Å., 1987. 'Siting of groundwater dams for rural water supply in developing countries—hydrogeological and planning aspects, part 1: regional study in south India'. (In print). The Royal Institute of Technology, Stockholm.

Nilsson, Å,; Sivanappan, R.K.; 1985. *Utilisation of dams for groundwater recharge and storage in Coimbatore District, India. Project proposal.* Water Technology Centre, Coimbatore. 11 pp.

Nilsson, Å.; Sivanappan, R.K., 1986. *Hydrological and water engineering aspects of the Ayyalur Interface Forestry Project, Tamil Nadu.* SB Press, Trivandrum, India. 30 pp.

Nissen-Petersen, E., 1982. *Rain catchment and water supply in ruralAfrica: a manual.* Hodder & Stoughton, Great Britain. 83 pp.

Oliveira, A.M.S.; Leite, C.A.G., 1984. *Tecnologias simples para aproveitamentos de pequeno porte dos recursos hidricos do semi-árido nordestino.* IPT, Divisào de Minas e Geologia Applicada. São Paulo. 83 pp.

Pavlin, B., 1973. 'Establishment of sub-surface dams and utilization of natural sub-surface barriers for realization of underground storages in the coastal karst spring zones and their protection against seawater intrusion'. In: *Trans 11th Int. Congress on Large Dams,* Vol.1, Madrid, pp.487–501.

Pompeu dos Santos, J.; Frangipani, A., 1978. 'Barragens submersasuma alternativa para o nordeste Brasileiro'. *Congresso Brasileiro de geologia de engenheira,* pp. 119–126.

Pozzi, R.; Benvenuti, G., 1979. 'Studio geologico applicato e geofisico per dighe subalvee nel distretto del Nogal (Somalia Settentrionale)'. *Memorie di Scienze Geologiche già Memorie degli Instituti di Geologia e mineralogia dell' Università di Padova,* Vol.XXXII, 33 pp.

Provisional Military Government of Socialist Ethiopia, 1984. *Remote sensing for water resources development—A demonstration and training study.* VIAK, Stockholm. 48 pp.

Raju, K.C.B., 1983. 'Sub-surface dams and its advantages'. In: *Proc. Seminar on Assessment, Development & Management of Ground Water Resources,* April 29–30, 1982, Central Ground Water Board, New Delhi, India.

Robaux, A., 1954. 'Les barrages souterraines'. *Terres et eaux,* Vol.6, No.23, pp. 23–27. Paris.

Sauermann, H.B., date unknown. 'Sand versus sun'. South-West Africa. 3 pp.

Schuyler, J.D., 1986. *Pacoima Dam, California. USGS 18th Annual Report,* Part IV, pp. 693–695.

Skibitzke, H.E.; Bennet, R.R.; da Costa, J.A.; Lewis, D.D.; Maddock, T. Jr., 1961. 'Symposium on history of development of water supply in an arid area in southwestern United States—Salt River Valley, Arizona'. In: *Groundwater in arid zones, Symposium of Athens,* 1961, Vol.2, *Int. Assoc. Sci. Hydrology Pub.,* pp. 706–742.

Slichter, 1902. 'Sub-surface dams'. *USGS Water Supply and Irrigation Papers,* No.67, pp. 76–78.

Stengel, H.W., 1968. *Wasserspeicherung in den sanden eines riviers. Wissenschaftliche Forschung in Südwestafrika (7. Folge).* John Meinert (Pty) Ltd., Windhoek, S.W.A., 54 pp.

Sundborg, A., 1982. 'Erosion and sedimentation processes'. In: *Sedimentation Problems in River Basins,* IHP Project 5.3, UNESCO, Paris.

Sykes, G.G., 1937. 'Desert water tanks'. *Engineering News Record.* July 1, 1937.

Sörlie, J.E., 1978. 'Water conservation techniques proposed in North Turkana, Kenya'. *Hydrology in Developing Countries, Nordic IHP Report No.2,* National Committees for the International Hydrological Programme in Denmark, Finland and Sweden. pp. 99–112.

Tanganyika Territory Geological Survey Department, 1928. Annual Report, 1928, pp.34–36.

Taylor, G.C., 1984. 'Weathered hard rocks'. In: *Ground Water in Hard Rocks,* IHP Report No.33, UNESCO, Paris.

The American City, 1974. 'Artificial aquifer stops storm pollution'. *The American City,* May 1974. p. 106.

The Hindu, 1986. 'Novel method to harness sub-soil water'. *The Hindu,* Friday, July 25, 1986.

The Hindu, 1987. 'Three more sub-surface dams in A.P. by May'. *The Hindu,* 17.2.1987. 1 p.

Tröften, P.F., 1982. Personal communication.

UNESCO, 1984. *Project Newsletter No.2. Major regional project on the rational utilisation and conservation of water resources of rural areas of Africa (south of the Sahara).* Paris, pp. 5, 6, 7 & 10.

United Nations, 1973. *Groundwater in Africa.* UN Publication, Sales No.E.71.II. A.16., New York, 179 pp.

Veja, 1984. 'Com os pés no sertão. Surgem nos laboratories soluçoes simples e eficazes para enfrentar o clima instável do Nordeste'. *Veja,* 2 de maio, 1984.

Verboom, W.C., data unknown. *Conservation notes for field staff in Zambia, III Water Conservation*. Ministry of Rural Development, Lusaka. 12 pp.

Wade, F.B., 1927. 'Water supplies in the region between Tabora and Speke Gulf. *Tanganyika Territory, Bulletins of the Geological Survey Department, 1927*. London. 19 pp.

Werner, V.; Haze, W., 1982. Machakos Integrated Development Programme, Kenya. Personal communication.

White, G.F. (ed), 1956. The future of arid lands'. Papers and Recommendations from the *International Arid Lands Meeting*. Publication No.43 of the American Association for the Advancement of Science, Washington. 453 pp.

Willis, D.L. (date unknown). 'Sub-surface groundwater reservoir for the City of Newark, Delaware: a concept for water salvage'.

Wipplinger, O., 1958. *The storage of water in sand*. South-West Africa Administration, Water Affairs Branch, 1958. 107 pp.

Wipplinger, O., 1961. 'Deterioration of catchment yields in arid regions, its causes and possible remedial measures'. Publication No.66, *Inter-African Conference on Hydrology*, Nairobi, 1961. pp. 281–289.

Wipplinger, O., 1965. 'Hidrologiese oorwegings by die ontwerp van sandstudamme'. *S.W.A. Boer/Farmer*, 16 August 1965, pp. 11–13.

Wipplinger, O., 1974. 'Sand storage dams in South-West Africa'. *Die Siviele Ingenieur in Suid-Africa*, April 1974, pp. 135–136.

Wipplinger, O., 1982. 'Water storage in semi-arid regions'. Unpublished paper. 30 pp.

Wipplinger, O., 1984a. 'Updating of records and methods'. Unpublished paper. 4 pp.

Wipplinger, O., 1984b. Personal communication.

Wipplinger, O., undated. 'Note on the Burger Beaumont method'. Unpublished paper. 1 p.

World Water, 1984. 'Swedish techniques aid Bolivians'. September, 1984. pp. 32–33.